BIG DATA

The Next Giant Step

Saeid Jamali

Saeid Jamali has researched the field of IoT and big data analysis as part of his degree. He is also the founder of the intellithing research group which was formed in 2017 to focus on innovating current technologies as well as creating new technologies that save lives and help humans live better.

An entrepreneur, an engineer, or a researcher?
A little bit of all.

IG: @saeid.jamali

E-mail: saeid_jamali@live.com

BIG DATA

The Next Giant Step

Contents

CONTENTS

TABLE OF FIGURES

GLOSSARY OF TERMS

SDDAF	Smart Distributed Data Analytics Framework
IoT	Internet of Things
DAS	Data analytics framework
ESB	Enterprise Service Bus
ML	Machine Learning
I/O	Input / output

INTRODUCTION

The massive increasing number of IoT devices creates new challenges regarding processing the data produced by these devices. In the near future, in the era of big data, humans will be facing petabytes of data produced by IoT devices in small time intervals. However, the devices are unable to process the huge amount of data by themselves. Furthermore, even the attempt to transfer the data to a centralized data centre is equivalent to a broken water dam which cannot be controlled in any way. This book introduces you to big data and emphasizes the importance of it. I explain why big data can be humans' saviour and save our extinction, and, on the other hand, how it could be used with bad intentions. In later chapters, I will introduce and explain how I build a big data analytics framework that uses big data to our advantage and makes humans' life better and easier.

The project is a proposal and implementation of a smart distributed data analytics framework that employs edge servers to pre-process the data on local gateways. The framework uses various machine learning algorithms which predicts the future based on the events that happened in the past. As a result, the data is not removed upon generation but instead, it is analysed with a machine learning algorithm which can solve complex scenarios that are not easy to solve for humans.

1. WHAT IS BIG DATA

There are many different definitions of big data, however, this explanation from Allister Heath from *Telegraph* was the easiest to understand when I first started to research this topic.

"Big data, a perfect example of the latter, is going to be a fantastic boon. Compiled from the digital trail left by web searches, credit card payments, and smartphones, it will transform productivity and consumer choice, and kick-start Western economies that have been in a rut for the best part of a decade. It will drive dramatic improvements in healthcare, education, and mobility, and allow us to live longer and better lives."

You understand it correct, big data is nothing but leftover from the digital world and we are talking about a huge amount of it; I like to say it is called big because the amount of the digital leftover is increasing at a high rate that no computer can process it. Fortunately, unlike the real world, we can delete all the leftover without being worried about environmental damages or any other harm at all. It is probably the easiest way to deal with the leftover because we have no commercial technology to make use of big data.

This was exactly the point when a lightbulb went off in my head, which inspired me and many people before me spend a few years of our lives focusing on answering these questions; what if we could make use of big data? And if we could, how could we possibly use it and why would we want to use it at all?

A clear view

Big data is normally referred to as a huge amount of data that is generated in the following categories.

- Traditional enterprise data including customer information, web store transactions, and general financial logs

- Machine-generated data including sensor data, weblogs, smart meter, IoT generated data, and other equipment logs

- Social data including customer feedback streams, and other social media frameworks such as Facebook and Twitter.

Key Parameters

Although volume is the most noticeable parameter, it is not the only characteristic of big data. In addition, four key characteristics define big data as described below.

- Volume: Machine-generated data in a company can produce large quantities of data. For example, a company producing sample data at a rate of 10TB of data in 30 minutes with thousands of branches across the world can run into petabytes of data in a day. This becomes more realistic, as connected IoT devices will increase to 50 billion devices by 2020 according to Cisco approximations (cited in Shah and Yaqoob, 2016). These IoT devices are devices such as heaters, fridges, engines, wind turbo, etc.

- Velocity: The social media stream is not as large as machine-generated data, however, it contains information, opinions, and relationships valuable to customer relationship management.

- Variety: variety in data format

- Value: The values of different data varies. There might be valuable information hidden among useless data: This is particularly important to identify valuable data to extract it for analysis purposes.

Difficulties

After reading the parameters, you probably have a better idea of why it is not very easy to use or process big data. Apart from the volume, it is generated from different sources with different data formats such as your smart meter, social media, and machine-generated, for example, and some do not even have any data format at all. To top this off, we never know which sets of data are actually useful and which sets are useless. A good analogy for better understanding this problem is trying to find a lost ring in an ocean. Furthermore, big data is not useful on its own as it is a combination of a variety of formats from different sources that are generally unusable for humans. In addition, it requires a system to identify the valuable data among all other data to analyse the valuable part and make use of it. I would like to end the difficulties here, but there are many other obstacles in the way of processing big data. Trying to process big data is equivalent to trying to stop a flood caused by a broken dam with your hands. Clearly, the flood washes everything on its way, a similar thing happens if one tries to process big data with traditional computers—they simply overload within a few seconds.

2. THE SAVIOUR

I believe big data is the next giant step that humans will take in history, and I have reasons to believe this. Big data is the next big thing that will happen after the Internet and computers. It will make humans' lives easier and longer.

It will make humans more technologically advanced, a world that is ruled by advanced humans who are resistant to diseases and illnesses.

Big data is the key to exploring outer space. Big data will help our future generation to step out of the solar system. It will allow humans to predict the future and adjust their lives accordingly. In another word, if human extinction was to happen, big data would be the saviour of humans.

I am not talking about science-fiction here, I am talking about science alone. All this seems imaginary to our mind in 2020, however, believe it or not, it is scientifically proven on a very small scale that big data has this potential. Proving this concept by the framework that I developed in my university laboratory was why I was awarded a degree in science and engineering. It was incredibly time consuming and difficult, which made me want to change my research area several times. However, the results cheered me up, and as small as it was, I proved that big data is extremely valuable.

It is hard to believe that the digital leftover has this massive potential. I believe what makes big data capable of all that is the fact that there is no rhythm in it. It is produced from a variety of sources from all around the planet with no structure or limitation. Furthermore, to the contrary, this is exactly why it is difficult for humans to make sense of it.

Big data—the new gold, a resource

There will be 50 billion IoT devices connected to the internet by the end of 2020 as Cisco predicted many years ago. When I was doing my research, it seemed like a future far away, but I am now writing this book in the beginning of 2020. The future is already here.

These 50 billion devices are not mobile devices or tablets, I am talking about 50 billion smart things that are connected to the internet (IoT devices) and produce data at a huge rate every second. I remember my first proposal to deal with this massive growth of data production was to destroy them upon generation. I clearly remember the project supervisor who told me data is the new gold. 'You wouldn't destroy gold, would you?' 'No,' I'd replied. 'Then don't even think of destroying data as a solution,' he'd said. At the time, I was confused as to why he was comparing data to gold, but in six months' time, I was the one referring to big data as the new gold.

Big data is like raw natural resources, or at least I'd like to compare it to natural resources; I am sure there was a time when humans didn't know what refined oil and coal were. However, the time came when we learned how to refine the raw resources and learned how to keep our homes warm and streets lit by using refined natural resources. While humans thought keeping themselves warm was the only benefit, the time came when manufacturers were fuelled, so we manufactured things we could never think of. We manufactured four-wheeled wagons, called them cars, and fuelled them with refined resources. We made trains, fuelled aircraft, fuelled spaceships, and went to the moon. It all started by learning how to refine natural resources. I would like to think of big data as a digital resource that is not refined yet. We are in the early stage of refining this resource, so don't be surprised when I say big data will help our future generation to step out of the solar system.

What do we know so far

Researchers are beginning to notice big data, and more people are talking about this every day. When I first started researching this topic, there were extremely limited resources available, and every resource or researcher had their own version of defining it. It took me an incredibly long time just to fully understand what I was looking for or what big data was. When I was going through the work of previous researchers at the beginning of my research, I came across a couple of scientific articles that could not define big data, so they simply said there is no best way to describe it yet, or there is no correct way to describe it. Nowadays, in a matter of a few years, resources are becoming more unified when they talk about big data. There are more articles and journals available, and a single google search brings up numerous videos and seminars that truly explain big data. This proves even more that big data is the new gold, as it is clearly catching a lot of eyes.

A few simple concepts have experimented with big data. I will talk about them in later sections in more detail. We know big data is valuable, and we know the traditional computer processing power is not enough to make use of big data. As we said, trying to process big data is like trying to stop a flood caused by a broken dam with hands. Even if we try to process big data by a cluster of supercomputers, we run into problems.

Let me flashback to our oil example again. There came a point when we knew we had a natural resource; we knew we had to refine it, and all we needed was an effective way to refine the resource. A similar thing applies to big data, we know it exists, we know how we can use it, or, more precisely, we know just enough to start experiments, and we are working on the most effective way of processing it.

When I picked up the topic, the researchers were already halfway through researching how big data can be used. Therefore, I started by researching how I wanted to use it and how I want to process big data. As a result, I developed a framework that I call Smart Distributed Data Analytics Framework, which I will explain step by step in later chapters on how I built it and what was going through my mind during its construction. The only regret I have is that I called it smart instead of intelligent. I would be happier if it was called Intelligent Distributed Data Analytics Framework (IDDAF). It may not seem like it, but the difference is huge. Smart is more pre-programmed and logical and less to do with artificial intelligence. The exact reason I picked the term smart was because I was going to keep away from the AI side of it to make things easier, but once I dived in it, I had to bring the best out of it, so I empowered it with machine learning algorithms. The framework ended up being intelligent, but with the term smart in its title.

Data Analytics

Big data is a useless digital leftover on its own. It becomes valuable if we correctly analyse and extract information that is actually useful. Analysing big data is a huge challenge as many aspects of it need consideration, such as networking, storage, format conversion, data integration, noise filtering, and privacy. For example, if we again compare big data to a broken dam in terms of volume and flow, then how are we going to transfer it over the internet before even thinking of processing it? What is the plan for integrating the data? Unstructured data that might or might not even have a format. What sort of information are we going to look for? How do we filter noise and unwanted data from it? How will an analysis system be able to find valuable information that will help us improve our life? And even if we manage to go around all of it and process the data, where do we want to store it?

While I was trying to answer all those questions, I came across a research paper by Singh and Reddy published in 2014 that made me close my laptop for the day because I had been lost between all those problems when a new one came up. Their paper said; the data analytic frameworks of their time had a major issue—the more scalable they were, the less real-time processing power they had, and the more real-time processing power they had, the less scalable they were. Thus, they suggested to future researchers that the future frameworks should trigger a combination of highly scalable frameworks with high-performing, real-time processing power. The key elements required for big data analytics are: real-time and scalable; allowing the system to be future proof by easy development and the ability to process petabytes of data per second as they are being generated.

Later on that day, I decided to focus on combining scalability with high performing real-time processing power as well as introducing an infrastructure based on edge computing to further enhance the framework.

What problems can it solve?

Big data analysis is currently being used to predict the future, based on the events that happened in the past. Let us have a closer look at some examples. A train connected to the internet generates logs and leaves trails of data behind as it goes forward. The data might be unstructured and unrecognisable, but data analytics can collect and analyse this data and inform us that based on the events in the past and current data that is being generated, the train is about to break down. It will be able to specify why or which part is about to cause the failure. All by analysing the data that we called useless earlier. This is because the machine learning of the analysis can analyse and learn from the data.

Another example is that, a corporation that can analyse its historical data and the data that's being generated. The analytics result can make important decisions for business growth that is far more accurate and precise than an experienced CEO. All from leftover data such as website logs, transactions logs, smart meter leftover trials and other unwanted digital latter.

Big data analytics can be your financial advisor and make precise financial decisions for you by analysing your historical leftover data such as your social media, transactions, web search trails, etc. Every single transaction you had and every single spend pattern throughout your whole life can easily be analysed by an analytics framework to first, learn you and your behaviour, and second, to suggest where you should save and where you should invest.

Big data analysis can help you have a better lifestyle or save on energy consumption, all by analysing your historical data and behaviour which would be useless otherwise. The machine learning side of the analytics framework can identify weaknesses in your lifestyle and predict how they can affect your future. A framework can analyse your household data and suggest ways to improve efficiency of energy consumption within the household.

Let us have a look at another example; analysing big data in regard to housing and property can help you predict the future price fluctuations with a specific time and date of the occurrence. The more data it analyses, the more accurate it gets, and the more it learns, the better it can predict the future. I other words, it predicts future events based on historical data and events in the past that are meaningless to humans.

How does it learn from historical data?

Let us have a closer look to find out exactly how big data analysis works. What does it mean when I say the framework learns from the data? Imagine a warehouse that has a natural gas valve. If someone tells you the main valve of natural gas has been left open for a while and airways were blocked, the first thing you think of is a massive explosion that burns everything to the ground. Thus, the very first action you take is to reduce the chance of explosion by shutting the valve and opening doors and windows. This is your brain making predictions and assumes the outcome will be an explosion and fire. Your brain is making predictions based on hundreds of other similar scenarios. This is because your brain has analysed and learnt this data throughout years of observing similar situations. In almost every scenario that you have heard, you have seen, or even that your subconscious picked up without you realising it, the situation ends in fire and destruction. Your brain is correct to predict and make you rush to take actions such as reducing the chance of fire without the need to think.

Now, let's apply the same example in the digital world and big data. In the train example, the big data analysis will analyse the behaviour of the train and make predictions and assumptions based on that, just like the warehouse example. For example, Since the beginning, every time the train has entered a certain railway, it encountered technical difficulties, so if the train enters the same railway again, our logic can predict that it will encounter technical difficulties. This is simple logic that our brain can process, but when it comes to big data analysis, the details are remarkable. Don't forget, big data is a historical data of that particular train since it was made. Data of every single component under different circumstances such as the weather. For example, how a single screw of the engine responded when the train was going straight at a certain speed while the weather was cold. On the other hand, how a single screw of the engine responded when the train took a turn at a certain speed while the weather was cold. Now, imagine we can change this all day—different weather, different component, different speed, different railway, etc. Bear in mind, this set of data is being produced every second for every single component. Now imagine the data is available since the train has started to operate, let's say 10 years ago. Furthermore, this train is not the only train as there are probably thousands of other trains that produce the same data since the start of their operation. Big data analytics framework can go through all that data from all of the trains and make sense out of that, hence; it can predict future events based on the events that happened in the past.

Our brain, unlike big data analytics, is simply not capable of processing this huge amount of data to process and learn from it, but if we could process and learn, it would be as simple as our warehouse example when your logic predicted a fire or explosion based on all the events in the past.

Machine Learning

Machine learning is a key element in data analytics, and that is why big data analytics is extremely precise, because machine learning algorithms let the computers learn the data as they process it. Just like humans learning a new skill, the only difference is, machine learning learns and make decisions in less time with more accurate results. Machine learning is an application of artificial intelligence that not only makes a decision based on processed data in this case, big data but also learns the information the same way a human learns, and it becomes more intelligent as it learns more. The algorithms are normally created to simulate the human brain in terms of learning. Can big data be the start of super-intelligent robots? That is a topic for another book.

3. DANGERS OF BIG DATA

As good as big data sounds so far, it can be misused in ways that invade people's privacy, and it can turn into something dangerous if it gets in the wrong hands. Big data analysis must be regulated internationally when the time for commercial use comes. Analysing big data is not always as good as it sounds because if misused, it can have the opposite effect of the positive and useful intentions set out here. There is nothing wrong with big data itself, however, I believe strict regulations must be in place before we decide to take the next step and use big data in everyday life. The issues with privacy must be resolved before even attempting to commercialise the use of technology. We are living in a word where big companies such as Google and Facebook have already started collecting and using our personal data to their advantage for business growth purposes. Imagine if they are given this technology. Or imagine if governments start to use this technology to constantly manipulate us. The bad news is, those companies have already started to use big data and there are no regulations in place at all.

Keep big data away from politicians

I am talking about 10 years from now, this technology must be regulated the same way nuclear facilities are regulated. The power of big data can easily take democracy away from us if misused. Before I share with you a few ways I believe big data can be misused, I'd like to mention that there can be 100 other ways that we do not know yet.

Manipulating an election result has never been easier. Imagine if governments predict your future vote in an election as well as finding the reason you are voting for that particular party with big data analysis all by analysing your historical data including every movement, behaviour, and any data you have produced since birth. The rest is even easier, all they have to do is make personalised advertisements recommended by artificial intelligence to trigger your subconscious and change your mind or ensure your decision remains the same throughout the election with the same method.

We could be living in a society that gives us no choice in decision making at all, where decisions are made for us by machines or manipulated by the governments. This is the most dangerous of all, a world that is ruled by intelligent machines while we are kept in the delusion of having a choice. I won't continue the topic of machine learning, although it is intact with big data, the topic falls out of the scope of this book. However, I want to finish this with my experience during my research. when I was doing my research about machine learning and how I could use it in my data analysis framework, I came across an abundance of research papers that said the following at the end of their research; "to the future researcher, please be cautious with the topic of machine learning. Remember, computers are to serve humans, not humans to serve computers." This really touched me, and I could instantly imagine a future ruled by robots just like what I saw on TV when I was a kid.

Kill the witch

Why are we developing a technology that could be dangerous? Should we stop the development of big data analysis? My answer is no. The same way we do not stop the production of knives because they could be harmful. When the internet was created, we faced many similar issues, such as privacy, however, with correct controls and regulations, there will be no dangers associated with it.

4. PREPARATION FOR MAKING A FRAMEWORK

This part is the start of my adventure in building and developing a system that actually works. The experience of building this data analytics is the greatest experience of my life. I am thankful every day that I had the opportunity to work on this topic. At the same time, this period of time was one of the hardest times of my life, if not the hardest. I was facing challenges, constant failure, and personal problems; so much pressure that it truly made me feel at least 5 years older. To be quite honest, big data was not love at first sight for me. On the other hand, I fell in love with this topic once I was halfway through. That was when I truly started to understand and appreciate the topic. At first, it seemed rather straight forward, and this probably was the main reason I chose the topic—so I could earn my degree as easily as possible.

All I had to do was assemble a few components that already existed. I was clearly wrong, as the problem was more than assembling a few components. The more I dived in it, the more I drowned. Stressful nights and days followed, as every day that I failed was a day wasted, and I was one day closer to my deadlines. I tried every single possible way to get the system up and running, but I constantly failed. I woke up knowing I was about to fail; I was about to have a day full of failure, anger, stress, and disappointment. However, I knew something else as well, it wasn't about the degree or a finding a job anymore. It was about science, it was about me standing in front of everyone who doubted me to prove my point, it was about big data itself.

My secret to success was changing my attitude. A simple solution that changed my life. All I had to do was change my attitude. I realized the only thing that was holding me back was the fear of failure. Because every time I failed, I felt like the word came to an end, and this continuous torture was tearing me apart. This fear was holding me back. I was frustrated and stressed because I had to live in my fear, the fear of failure. I made no significant progress until I decided to face the fear of failure. I woke up the day after, knowing what I wanted to do. I was dedicated to fail. As crazy as it sounds, I wanted to go toward it rather than running away from it. Facing what stopped me from doing new things because what if I fail?

I remembered the times when I dreamed of studying computers and networking as a kid. As a teenager, I woke with the dream of someday becoming a professional in the field of computers. This re-inspired me because I realised—I was living my dreams. I was doing what I'd dreamed of doing as a kid, and I was stressed about it. What I was quite sure of was that, if anything, this should not be stressful at all. Focusing on the enjoyment of what I was doing really changed my mood. There was no failure anymore, there was only me doing what I enjoyed the most. The biggest lesson I learnt was to enjoy my moments and to have fun doing what I was doing. This is the secret to success, and I am sure, as long as we are enjoying what we do, success will follow.

If I failed, the worst-case scenario was that nothing would happen. If the results were instantly positive, it would be amazing, and if not, the worst was that nothing would happen. It wasn't even failure, it was me gaining experience while doing something fun.

After a while, I realized something strange was happening to me, I was no longer afraid of failure, or more accurately, I wasn't even thinking about failure. I was working on the project with the mindset that every time things didn't work; I was simply gaining experience, and this failure monster didn't exist for me anymore.

Early days

It all started from the day when someone who previously had supervised me in other projects talked about the concept of big data with me. We had to find someone to supervise us, and the topic we picked should be somehow related to our supervisor's field of research. When I spoke to the same person who originally told me about big data, he brought up the topic of big data analysis as a comprehensive framework. It seemed easy enough to start, although I had no clue what it really meant then.

I sent a proposal in regard to smart distributed big data analysis, which was accepted by my supervisor, it was then passed to the relevant department that arranged an interview to ensure my idea was worth spending time on. After the interview was the beginning of my stresses. Thinking about it day and night, whether or not I was going to get go-ahead. In about a week, I received an email from them recommending a few changes in my proposal but, overall, I was given the go-ahead. The next step was to prepare a presentation for them, to talk about what technologies were currently out there, what sort of issues they had and how I want to tackle the issues.

It didn't take long for me to prepare the presentation, and I was confident that I would succeed in this stage, just like other stages. The day arrived, I walked into the room and loaded my presentation to present my proposal in front of people who had a research background in the field of big data. While I was doing my presentation, I was thinking to myself—how could anyone possibly not like the idea. When I finished, the person who was supposed to judge me started his sentence by saying "nonsense". He said, "Young man, I spent the majority of my career researching this discipline. What you are saying makes no sense. You don't know what you want to do. You want to solve a problem, but you don't really understand the problem". His rather harsh comments ruined my self-confidence. I felt like I failed before I even began. I was extremely upset, but I needed a few days to really understand his point. He was right, I didn't know what I was going to do. I barely knew what big data was. How was I going to solve a problem without knowing the topic and problems associated with it? His harsh comments were my wakeup call, but the younger version of me was more dedicated to getting this done just so he could show those who doubted him he could do it.

So, I rescheduled the presentation and started to work on it. My daily routine became focused. I woke up every day at 5 am, worked on the project, went to work, and came back home and worked on my research again until 1:00 am. Considering I had no break during the day, I had the best nights of sleep at that time. I had only about 3 to 4 hours sleep with the hopes that it would soon be over. That was the biggest lie I ever told myself, as this lifestyle lasted for about a year throughout the project.

For the second presentation, I had a true understanding of the topic, as I had researched the majority of the works out there before myself, and I knew what I was going to do, I was going to address issues in regard to reliability, real-time processing, network traffic, and decision-making. I also knew what I was going to solve, I was going to solve the main problem that data analytics frameworks were facing which was combining high-scalable frameworks with high-performing, real-time processing frameworks through running various algorithmic components. This time, I had a project plan and fully structured stages of tackling the project, ethic checklist, cost estimation, a full risk assessment of the project, and a Gantt chart.

The second presentation went well, and I got to continue my project.

My novel contributions to science

I guess dreams do come true. There were days when I looked at university students and wondered if I could ever get an academic education since my broken English and my immigration status had held me back from entering university for years, and now I was talking about my contributions to science.

My project contributes to computer sciences and data analysis in the following ways. The topics below are some of the issues that the data analysis systems were facing.

• Reducing processing demand from centralized servers by introducing edge servers (a new layout of edge computing) to analyse data from sources that do not have the processing power for analysing their own generated data, such as smart meters or other smart things (IoT devices).

• Introducing a framework that is built using multiple components on top of a single framework which makes it scalable with real-time processing power (current technologies are either scalable or real-time).

• Addressing issues such as noise, filtering, and network traffic by pre-processing data on the edge of the local gateway (current methods suffer from excessive network traffic and possible noise in data which makes machine learning results unreliable).

All of the above is achieved through a precise implementation and a protocol that ensures the smooth operation of the implementation.

Literature Review

I did the partial literature review before my second presentation and completed it shortly before I began working in the laboratory. Literature review is the part of research when a researcher goes through previous research papers to ensure his work is unique and nobody else has created the work before to ensure their research is novel and to find out what is out there and what problems the current technologies suffer from so the researcher is up-to-date with the most recent technologies and researches. I will share part of my literature review in an easy to understand format. The word "et al." is used in scientific articles to refer to an article that has more than two writers or researchers, the main writer is mentioned followed by "et al." I will keep this as it is.

Edge Computing: Vision and Challenges (Shi et al., 2016)

Shi et al. start with describing the concept of edge computing and justifies as to why edge computing is essential. In general, Shi et al. believe that by 2019, the amount of data produced by internet users will reach up to 500 zettabytes as estimated by Cisco global cloud index. Moreover, there will be 50 billion devices producing data by 2020. A huge amount of the data is produced fairly recently, as devices are not only consumers anymore but producers as well. Furthermore, it defines the general idea of edge computing as; "Edge computing refers to the enabling technologies allowing computation to be performed at the edge of the network, on downstream data on behalf of cloud services and upstream data on behalf of IoT services. Here we define "edge" as any computing and network resources along the path between data sources and cloud data centres." (Shi et al., 2016:638)

The journal continues on, explaining the use of edge computing in analytics systems such as video analytics on page 639. It explains the use of edge computing in an analytics environment by giving an example of facial detection cameras, which indeed is a common and convincing example of edge computing. In the past, facial detection cameras were designed to record videos and stream the data continuously to a central datacentre, and the streamed data would be analysed for detecting the face. However, edge computing allows the cameras to process the data as they go and only contact the server when the target is detected. This is achieved by integrating the camera with a microcontroller that processes the video. The three main disadvantages of the traditional way that is mentioned in the journal is, first, the latency caused by sending the data over the network, second is the increased network traffic, and third, analysing a vaster amount of data from several cameras takes longer.

- However, the journal outlines a few problems that edge computing is suffering from.

- The details of data will be hidden, which affects the usability of the data

- If too much raw data is filtered, some applications and machines could not learn enough

- Data reported by the edge is not very reliable due to the low precision of sensors

To summarize the journal, by 2020, it is predicted that 50 billion devices will be on the network. These devices are not just consumers but producers as well, so, data generation is growing more and more with more devices connected to the internet. The solution to cope with this massive traffic is to reduce the data generated by using the concept of edge computing which allows things or devices on the edge to have processing ability. However, there are existing issues in the current implementations.

Big data analytics: a survey (Tsai et al., 2015)

Tsai et al. have researched the topic of big data analytics from a variety of sources before writing the journal. They have also included issues that are open for further development. The journal explains that the era of big data is ahead, however, the traditional data analytics may not be able to process such a massive amount of data. Furthermore, the journal focuses on current technologies and methods used in big data analytics followed by giving open issues that need further research. Tsai et al. explain that the problem of processing big data still exists, while the age of big data is ahead. In addition, big data is described as large-scaled data that current systems or methods are unable to process because, in the era of big data, the data will be too big to be processed by a single machine. Moreover, most traditional methods of data analytics developed for a centralized data analysis will be useless (Fisher et al., cited in Tsai et al 2015).

Tsai et al. define the following issues that the current systems are suffering from and need improvement.

- Communication between systems, including those with different data systems

- The cost of communications (e.g. sending data from a node in Asia to an analytics datacentre in the USA costs more)

- How to avoid excessive processing loads of the analytics system

- The issue of noise, an outlier, incomplete, and inconsistent data in traditional data mining

- Privacy and security concerns because systems cannot guarantee that the results of analysed data will not be accessed by other people

To summarize, the age of big data is ahead of humans. This means large-scaled data that are too big to be processed by the current analytics method. In addition, the current structure of centralized data analysis will not be able to cope with big data.

A survey on frameworks for big data analytics (Singh and Reddy, 2014)

The aim of (Singh and Reddy) is to provide an in-depth analysis of different frameworks, both hardware and software, currently available for big data analytics system. This journal compares different frameworks currently available for an analytics system with parameters such as scalability, data I/O performance, fault tolerance, real-time processing, data size support and iterative tasks support in mind. (Singh and Reddy) however, highlight their findings on the main issue of current frameworks. The higher scalability the frameworks have, the less real-time processing power they have. Furthermore, the journal suggests that future research should trigger the combination of highly scalable frameworks with high performing real-time processing frameworks by running various algorithmic components.

Big Data: A Survey (Chen, Mao and Liu, 2014)

The purpose of this paper is to review the background of big data and other related technologies. Chen et al. outline the four phases of the value chain of big data, i.e., data generation, data acquisition, data storage, and data analysis. Each phase is reviewed separately followed by a discussion on technical challenges.

Some of the most important open issues that Chen et al. pointed out are listed below.

- Format conversion of big data: so it can be communicated from various sources

- Big data transmission: as it incurs high costs

- Real-time performance: as it is a major problem in many application scenarios

- Processing of big data: as processing arises from traditional data analysis

- Searching big data: including distributed searching

- Data security and privacy

- Ability to produce the analysed data in the form of a visualized report (user-friendly display of results so it can be used effectively)

To summarize, Chen et al. believe that the most considerable research efforts are needed to improve the efficiency of the display, storage, and analysis of big data.

Networking for Big Data: A Survey (Yu et al., 2017)

Yu et al. first clarify the definition of networking for big data, followed by reviewing the current understanding of big data from different aspects such as formation, networking features, mathematical representation, and networking technologies. Eventually, the challenges from various perspectives are discussed. Some of the key difficulties that the current methods of data analytics are facing are as below.

- Heterogeneous network analysis

- Dynamic representation in networking for big data (Visualization techniques)

- Security and privacy

- Networking for big graph mining (how to mine such big data from various sources)

To summarize the journal, the era of big data is close, however, there are many new problems and issues with the current big data applications. Thus, it makes networking for big data a critical field to study in order to overcome problems with existing big data applications.

All of the writers above agree on similar problems that the current data analytics frameworks are facing. The table below categorizes all issues, followed by the proposed way to overcome the problems. As suggested by (Singh and Reddy) earlier, the proposed framework uses various components that work on top of a scalable open-source framework to overcome its weaknesses.

Current Issues	Ways to overcome
Reliability issues of edge systems (inaccurate data or noise)	Edge analytics servers that check data for accuracy and filtration
Communication between different nodes with different data format	Using integration components within the platform
Costs of communication (e.g one node in Asia and data centre in USA costs more)	Local edge analytics servers rather than centralized datacentre
Processing of massive data including real time processing	Processing data through processing components working on the top the platform. cooperating with edges devices so the amount of process is reduced

Security and privacy	Accessing information through API for individuals
Visualization	Visualization of data through a user-friendly graphical interface with visualization components
Decision Making	Machine Learning components

How I managed the project

A good idea is empowered by good management. An organisation or project will most certainly fail without good management in place. Before I even entered the laboratory, I wrote how I want to manage and plan the project on paper. I cannot emphasise how important it is to plan and manage a project or even a business, as this shortens the process of making or saving money, and implements the ideas in the most effective and efficient way.

Project management defines five processes that lead the project from start to finish: "initiation, planning, executing, monitoring & controlling, and closing". The reason I spent 4 months on project planning prior to starting the project is because of 5 very important key points.

1- Strategy alignment: it ensures what is being delivered is correct and will deliver real value for businesses.

2- Leadership: it provides leadership, vision, motivation, coaching, and inspiring the team members to do their best, or, in other words; it directs the project.

3- Achieving objectives: it ensures there is a precise plan for achieving objectives.

4- Process tracking: it ensures the plan is followed and the right people do the right thing at the right time.

5- Risk assessment: it ensures risks are assessed before becoming issues.

Initiation:

The base of the project is shaped in this stage by proposing a solution to the current issues surrounding current methods of data analysis. Furthermore, this is part of the project where aims and objectives are laid out. This is achieved by undertaking a series of research and analysing the original proposal to ensure the base of the project is shaped correctly.

Planning:

For managing time, costs, resources, and risk assessment, a plan is introduced to ensure the objectives are achieved in accordance with budget and resources in a specific period.

Execution:

Execution is the longest phase of the project. This phase is where all the findings are put into action for building the system. Moreover, all the objectives are executed step by step.

Monitoring and controlling:

In this phase, the project is constantly monitored and controlled to ensure it is on the right track and all the objectives are achieved step by step. Two methods of process tracking and communication management are used to ensure monitoring and controlling is always in place.

Closing:

This phase is to assemble and test the design using testbeds.

5. THE BEGINNING

I spent a lot of time to prepare, think, and imagine. This is my personality—I like to start things slowly but plan it ahead. Some people call me slow; I call myself strategic. I planned my next 20 steps, I imagined what every step would lead me to in different scenarios. This is my biggest recommendation to everyone—always plan all of your steps and execute them one by one rather than let's start it and see where it goes.

At this stage, I had a vision, I was going to develop an implementation or a protocol rather than building a hardware or software that does the analytics. An implementation that can easily be further developed. I needed to have a few things ready; a machine learning algorithm, a data analytics software with real-time processing power, and a way of implementing them. I started by coding a machine learning algorithm. The topic of artificial intelligence falls out of my study field, so it was challenging to code an algorithm that actually does the job to a high standard. It was not only challenging, but impossible to code it before the deadlines. The reason for that was because my initial vision was to create an implementation or a protocol, but my time was being wasted because machine learning should have been considered a tool for building the project and not the main focus. Although this constantly slowed me down, thankfully, my project management was strong enough to bring me back to the right track.

The beginning was the hardest because I didn't know where to start. Although I knew what I wanted and where I wanted to go with this, I really didn't know where to start. That first step is the hardest someone will take in their life toward their goals. I am thankful because this project changed my life and mindset. If it wasn't for this project, I would have never learnt that the first step is the hardest, but once you take that very first step, everything will follow smoothly. We humans normally have visions and goals, we want to achieve things, we want to earn things, and we want to complete things, but what stops the majority of us is just the first step. We humans decide to have the ideal life, whether it's a science project to complete or building a financial empire or even building our body, but what stops us from achieving them is only the first step. The interesting thing is that we start to blame everyone and make up excuses to justify the fact that we don't want to take the first step. The blames and excuses are endless; my university is not good, my dad wasn't rich and didn't give me enough, my genetics are not good, or we just come up with excuses such as; I can't do it today because my cat is alone, I will wait until some later time, I don't have the time now, and a multitude of other excuses as to why we don't want to take the first step. This project pushed me into taking the first step because there was a deadline. And I wanted my degree.

The first step

The first step for me was to actually do the things that I planned without being afraid of the outcome and without being worried about my top question 'what if it doesn't work'. Instead of trying to build things that are not the focus of my research topic, I used open source software that is highly robust and customisable, this little technique boosted me up all of a sudden from the person who felt he was behind to becoming the guy who was ahead of the game. This was my first step, customising open source software that is already out there to use to my advantage. After all, my project wasn't a software development, so wasting my time trying to develop software was a poor decision.

I came across an open source software called WSO2. A robust software that had all the features I was looking for. Customising Wso2 sounds easy, however, it took me a lot of effort to customise and prepare it for my implementation and protocol. Changes I made didn't work, and I didn't know why. Sometimes when things don't work, all you have to do is to step back, observe, and think, rather than constantly trying to make them work. I wholeheartedly believe this. I am the persistent person who keeps trying and trying and gets frustrated when things don't work, but once I acted against my nature and stepped back to observe, I could see the problem crystal clear.

The problem was simple, by customising multiple software, I was breaking their communication link at the same time. Easy enough to solve, but it took me a while to find out why. This is the thing about computers, fixing them is fine, but finding why they act strange is incredibly time consuming. When I say acting strange, I mean on a very low-level computing environment where there is only a series of binary zeros and ones. Every time I see a man complaining about how complicated it is to understand their other half, it makes me smile, as they clearly never came across an intelligent form that only communicates through a series of binary zeros and ones. 01110100 01110010 01111001 00100000 01110100 01101111 00100000 01110101 01101110 01100100 01100101 01110010 01110011 01110100 01100001 01101110 01100100 00100000 01110100 01101000 01101001 01110011 00101110.

6. MAIN SOFTWARE

I used a few main components to build the framework. The design is an implementation that is scalable because it is made of smaller components that can be developed as an individual software but work together as a system. The novelty, and what makes me the proudest, is the protocol that I developed so any data analytics framework with any components can be implemented in such a way that is capable of analysing big data.

The main components are IoT server, Data Analytics server, ESB server, Machine learning algorithm.

IoT server

- Ability to manage IoT devices, sensors, and capture data from them

- Connect devices and their data to larger enterprise's ecosystem

- Transform information into actionable insight in real-time

- Support for multi-tenancy

- Web-based management portal

- Extensible Architecture

- Allows optimization of network traffic by edge computing

implementation

The figure below illustrates the overview of WSO2 IoT server architecture

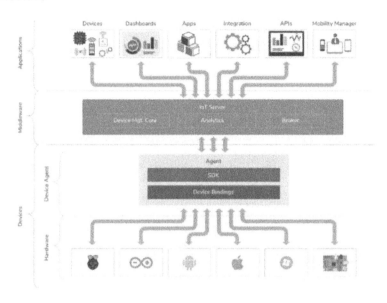

Figure 2 WSO2 IoT server core architecture

(Wso2.com, 2018)

WSO2 IoT server allows monitoring devices and data in real-time with the ability to define geofences. Furthermore, implementing data processing on local gateways is easy. In addition, it allows a series of performances on the edge of the network including passive/active monitoring of devices, pushing own rules and policies, use of complex event processing in real-time, perform batch analysis of historical data, declare multiple edge gateways, filtering data, and computing on the edge and generate alert and action. WSO2 IoT server is massively scalable and works seamlessly with other devices or WSO2 components. (Anon, n.d.). However, IoT server role in this system is to pre-process the data including filtration, integration, and edge computing implementation. To have real-time processing, IoT server is integrated with siddhi component which handles real-time processing.

The main reason for having IoT servers on the local gateways is to pre-process the data including filtration and integration of the data which is collected with different formats (the integration is mainly managed by ESB server). IoT servers are located on local gateways to pre-process or pre-analyse the data before they are sent to the main analytics server. Moreover, data is more reliable as noise and other irrelevant data is filtered. In addition, network traffic is controlled as the data is handled locally through these edge servers rather than transferring huge amounts of data over the network from one location to a centralised server.

Data Analytics server

The open source Stream Processor creates real-time, intelligent, actionable insights.

The figure below demonstrates three phases of collect, analyse, and action. Event to action phase occurs within milliseconds.

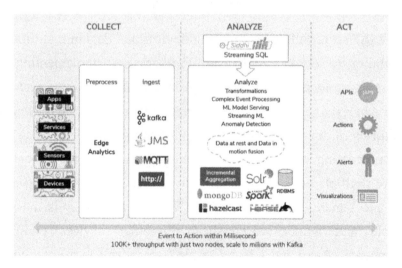

Figure 3 Data Analytics Server Events to action

(Wso2.com, 2018)

Some of the functionalities of DAS is listed below.

- Processing millions of events per second in real-time

- Investigates the past to predict the future

- Enables businesses to manage their rules and visualization output

- Can be combined with Siddhi and IoT server to handle the massive amount of data on the edge of the network

- Quick and fast development

- Some of the businesses that currently use DAS are below.

- Uber: Detects fraud in real-time processing over 400k events per second

- Transport for London: uses real-time streaming to create next generation transport systems

- United Airlines: improves passenger wait times and logistics via real-time IoT data and predictions

Data analytics server is the main analytic part of the system, which receives filtered data from IoT server for analysis purposes. DAS uses a machine learning algorithm so it can make decisions in real-time or predict the future based on events that happened in the past. The results of the analytics server will be stored in a database which then can be accessed by IoT devices which produced the data at the first place. The ultimate advantage of DAS is that it is scalable with real-time processing power through multiple components such as real-time processing Siddhi, machine learning component, and visualization component. Furthermore, many components can be added to the main data analytics software core with simple configurations.

ESB server

- 160+ ESB connectors across various categories, such as payments, CRM, ERP, social networks, or legacy systems

- Message formats & protocols: JSON, XML, SOAP

- Supports MSSQL, DB2, Oracle, OpenEdge, TerraData, MySQL, PostgreSQL/EnterpriseDB, H2, Derby, or any database with a JDBC driver

- Support for nested queries across data sources

- ESB Routing Support: header based, content-based, rule-based, and priority-based routing

- ESB ships with a built-in standard compliant, portable, interoperable message broker for guaranteed delivery of messages

- ESB is capable of providing sub-millisecond latency for high-throughput scenarios

The figure below illustrates the overview of ESB server.

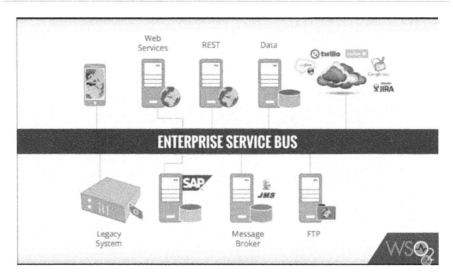

Figure 4WSO2 ESB Server

(Wso2.com, 2018)

Enterprise service bus acts as a bus system in between services and servers to enable different file formats and service to communicate seamlessly. Furthermore, because in the concept of data analysis data is collected from different file formats, different devices, and is passed through multiple servers with different functionality, it is essential to have a bus system that integrates applications, services, data, and processes across on-premise systems, the cloud, and the IoT. ESB enables migration between servers, public cloud, and private cloud.

Machine learning algorithm

Machine learning component takes data analysis to another level by allowing the system to predict the future based on the events that happened in the past. In addition, the data is used to make decisions for future problems.

The figure below demonstrates the overall view of the machine learning component.

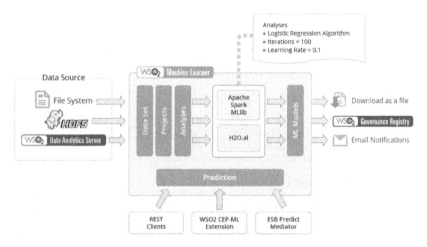

Figure 6 Machine learning architecture

(Wso2.com, 2018)

As the figure suggests, data sets are extracted from the file system and analytics server. This data is then passed to machine learner core which applies various machine learning algorithms to the data. Machine learning components use apache spark to analyse and build models using the chosen algorithm.

Laboratory Implementation

The architecture is implemented using the following network infrastructure.

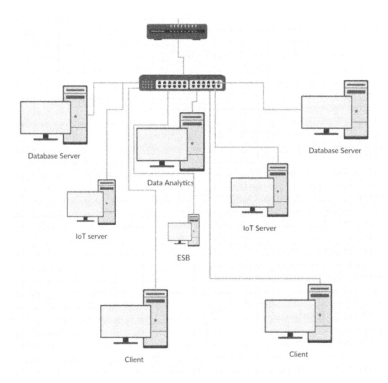

Figure 7 Network infrastructure

Using instructions in section 7, all computers are configured and connected to a switch which is then connected to a router. To illustrate a distributed computing environment in the implementation, all servers are configured on an individual virtual LAN on a Cisco switch, and the router is configured with Router_On_A_Stick. Furthermore, this creates the illusion that each individual server is on a different LAN.

7. RESULTS

It probably only took you and hour or two to get from the beginning chapter to the result chapter, but it took me three years to gain the knowledge of creating such a thing, including one full year of hard work of dedication and focus. As well as sleeping only three hours a day to having days with no break. One thing that kept me going was reminding myself how far I'd come and what my goal was. Every time I was exhausted, I went back to the beginning and did the things I did in the beginning. From watching videos that gave me motivation, to reading books and articles that excited me to study computer and networking technology. After all, this is what made me an engineer. There is no success without failure and hard work. Please remember; failure is simply you gaining experience so you can deal with the same situation next time.

The sweet taste of victory. There is nothing that feels better than the feeling when you put the last piece of a puzzle together and solve it. The moment that I had the system up and running and tested was one of the best moments of my life. I felt an extreme rash of dopamine and adrenaline through my whole body. I was screaming, shouting, and jumping up and down like a kid, and at the same time, I was fascinated by the results produced by the framework.

The first test was using historical weather data to predict the future (the time of testing which was the future relative to the data). I specifically chose weather data because it is generic. No sensitive data was involved, so I could rest assured there was no ethical issue related to the project, otherwise, it could conflict with the engineering code of ethics. The results were fascinating—the framework successfully predicted weather situations of the future (The time of the test which was future relative to the data). I myself was left with conflicting emotion. I wanted to be happy, but I was nervous, so I wanted to be nervous, but I was excited, but then again, I was happy but worried as it was bringing up the results. I was overwhelmed. I was shouting "it's working, it's actually working," and others around me in the lab, including the strict lab manager were looking at me with satisfaction and smile on their faces as if they were sharing the excitement with me.

I strongly believe big data will change the future of humanity. It will be the next giant step humans will take. We humans have the desire to be better and do better. We humans were originally preys, however, it didn't take long before we dominated the planet earth; we built civilizations, formed governments, and took the full control of the planet. The irresistible urge to be better didn't let us accept our destiny as weak preys and made us the dominant species. The same urge wants us to go beyond our planet, colonise other planets or even other galaxies. I strongly believe the key to achieving more is big data.

8. REFERENCES

BIBLIOGRAPHY

Heath, A. (2018). *'Big data' is the black gold of today. It's time for politicians to catch up*. [online] The Telegraph. Available at: http://www.telegraph.co.uk/news/2017/09/14/big-data-black-gold-today-time-politicians-catch/

Dijcks, J. (2013). *Oracle: Big Data for the Enterprise*. [ebook] Redwood Shore: Oracle Corporation, pp.3-4. Available at: http://www.oracle.com/us/products/database/big-data-for-enterprise-519135.pdf

Shah, S. and Yaqoob, I. (2016). A survey: Internet of Things (IOT) technologies, applications and challenges. *2016 IEEE Smart Energy Grid Engineering (SEGE)*.

Techopedia.com. (2018). *What is Project Planning? - Definition from Techopedia*. [online] Available at: https://www.techopedia.com/definition/14005/project-planning

eduCBA. (2018). *Project Plan vs Project Management Plan - Excited to Compare*. [online] Available at: https://www.educba.com/project-plan-vs-project-management-plan/

PM Study Circle. (2018). *Project Plan vs Project Management Plan*. [online] Available at: https://pmstudycircle.com/2012/01/project-plan-vs-project-management-plan/

2020projectmanagement.com. (2018). *10 Reasons why Project management matters Project Management*. [online] Available at:

http://2020projectmanagement.com/2015/10/10-reasons-why-project-management-matters/

Twago.com. (2018). *4 reasons why a project plan will make your life easier | twago blog*. [online] Available at: https://www.twago.com/blog/project-plan-makes-life-easier/

Bridges, J. (2018). *Project Planning v. Project Management - ProjectManager.com*. [online] ProjectManager.com. Available at: https://www.projectmanager.com/training/project-planning-vs-project-management-spot-the-difference

The Digital Project Manager. (2018). *Why is Project Management Important? - The Digital Project Manager*. [online] Available at: https://thedigitalprojectmanager.com/why-is-project-management-important/

Shi, W., Cao, J., Zhang, Q., Li, Y. and Xu, L. (2016). Edge Computing: Vision and Challenges. *IEEE Internet of Things Journal*, 3(5), pp.637-646.

Anon, (n.d.). *WSO2 IoT server*. [online] Available at: https://wso2.com/library/webinars/2017/09/5-cool-things-you-can-do-with-wso2-iot-https://wso2.com/library/webinars/2017/09/5-cool-things-you-can-do-with-wso2-iot-server/server/

Docs.oracle.com. (2018). *Installingthe JDK Software and Setting JAVA_HOME (Using the GlassFish ESB Installation CLI)*. [online] Available at: https://docs.oracle.com/cd/E19182-01/820-7851/inst_cli_jdk_javahome_t/ [Accessed 11 Apr. 2018].

Statistics Solutions. (n.d.). *What is Linear Regression? - Statistics Solutions*. [online] Available at: http://www.statisticssolutions.com/what-is-linear-regression/

Learningnetwork.cisco.com. (2014). Fundamentals of VLAN's - Router on a stick - 23481 - The Cisco Learning Network. [online] Available at: https://learningnetwork.cisco.com/docs/DOC-23481

REFERENCES

Wso2.com. (2018). Machine Learner. [online] Available at: https://wso2.com/products/machine-learner/.

Wso2.com. (2018). WSO2 Analytics. [online] Available at: https://wso2.com/analytics.

Wso2.com. (2018). WSO2 Enterprise Service Bus - The Only 100% Open Source ESB. [online] Available at: https://wso2.com/products/enterprise-service-bus/#Capabilities.

Shi, W., Cao, J., Zhang, Q., Li, Y. and Xu, L. (2016). Edge Computing: Vision and Challenges. IEEE Internet of Things Journal, 3(5), pp.637-646.

Tsai, C., Lai, C., Chao, H. and Vasilakos, A. (2015). Big data analytics: a survey. Journal of Big Data, 2(1).

Singh, D. and Reddy, C. (2014). A survey on platforms for big data analytics. Journal of Big Data, 2(1).

Chen, M., Mao, S. and Liu, Y. (2014). Big Data: A Survey. Mobile Networks and Applications, 19(2), pp.171-209.

Yu, S., Liu, M., Dou, W., Liu, X. and Zhou, S. (2017). Networking for Big Data: A Survey. IEEE Communications Surveys & Tutorials, 19(1), pp.531-549.

sources in the current document.

www.ingramcontent.com/pod-product-compliance
Lightning Source LLC
LaVergne TN
LVHW092031060326
832903LV00058B/511